HOW TO BE ANALYZED BY A NEUROTIC PSYCHOANALYST

HOW TO BE ANALYZED BY A NEUROTIC

NEW ENGLISH LIBRARY
TIMES MIRROR

PSYCHOANALYST

BY STEPHEN BAKER

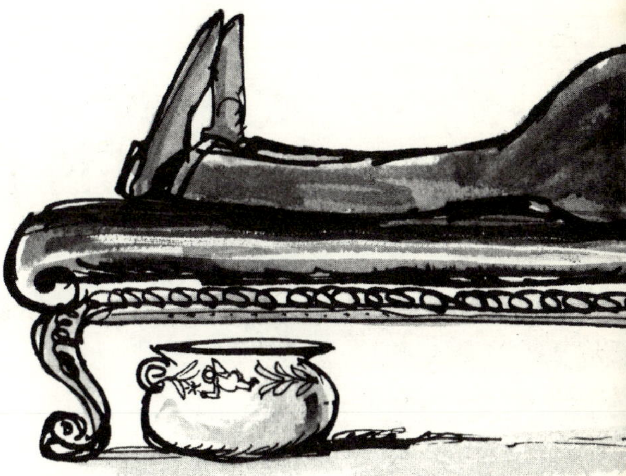

Cartoons by

JOHN HUEHNERGARTH

Dedicated to all psychoanalysts
with a sense of humor

First published in the United States of America by Doubleday & Co., Inc.
First published by New English Library 1971
Printed and bound in Great Britain by C. Tinling & Co. Ltd, Prescot.
45000751 0

CONTENTS

1

HOW TO FIND THE NEUROTIC PSYCHOANALYST JUST RIGHT FOR YOU

There are about 2500 psychoanalysts in this country. About 2500 are neurotic—a conservative estimate.

This is hardly surprising when you consider their way of life. Theirs is a demanding profession. Imagine listening to other people's problems all day long with barely enough time between sessions to pause for a drink or even go to the bathroom.

Fortunately, psychoanalysts are trained to deal expertly with all sorts of emotional disturbances, especially if they are their own. They simply talk things over with those who understand; namely, their patients and their own psychoanalysts.

Every psychoanalyst maintains a private therapist in whom he can confide.

This is an accepted practice in the profession, and an eminently practical one. The arrangement provides income to a fellow practitioner who then passes his fee on to his psychoanalyst, and so on.

Thus, the original investment eventually goes back to where it came from, keeping the money in circulation among friends and out of the hands of laymen.

The initial interview with your therapist is one of the most important; it is an opportunity to get to know him. You will be asked to take up space not on the couch but on a chair specially retained for just such an occasion across his desk.

This may be your first—and perhaps last—chance to observe his countenance at close range. Watch his facial expressions as he talks about his early childhood.

Do not be alarmed by his nervous tic; remember, he had a difficult childhood. In fact, he is still going through it.

Try to stay awake; listen to what he says. Then, and only then, decide whether or not you are qualified to help him resolve his various emotional problems.

How to recognize a psychoanalyst on sight. It is possible to tell much about him if you know what to look for. Watch for the following signs of professionalism: A reclining chair **(1)** to permit him to lean back far enough so as to be able to examine the ceiling. Within easy reach is his desk drawer **(2)** in which he keeps his sandwiches, a bottle opener, a fly swatter, piggy bank, dice, cordless electric shaver, erector set, waterpistol, roller skates, and a prospectus of a nudist colony just outside town. He is also the likely possessor of a notebook **(3)** which enables him to keep track of his monthly income.

No psychoanalyst is complete without his beard. Pull hard to confirm its authenticity.

Three basic types of psychoanalysts.

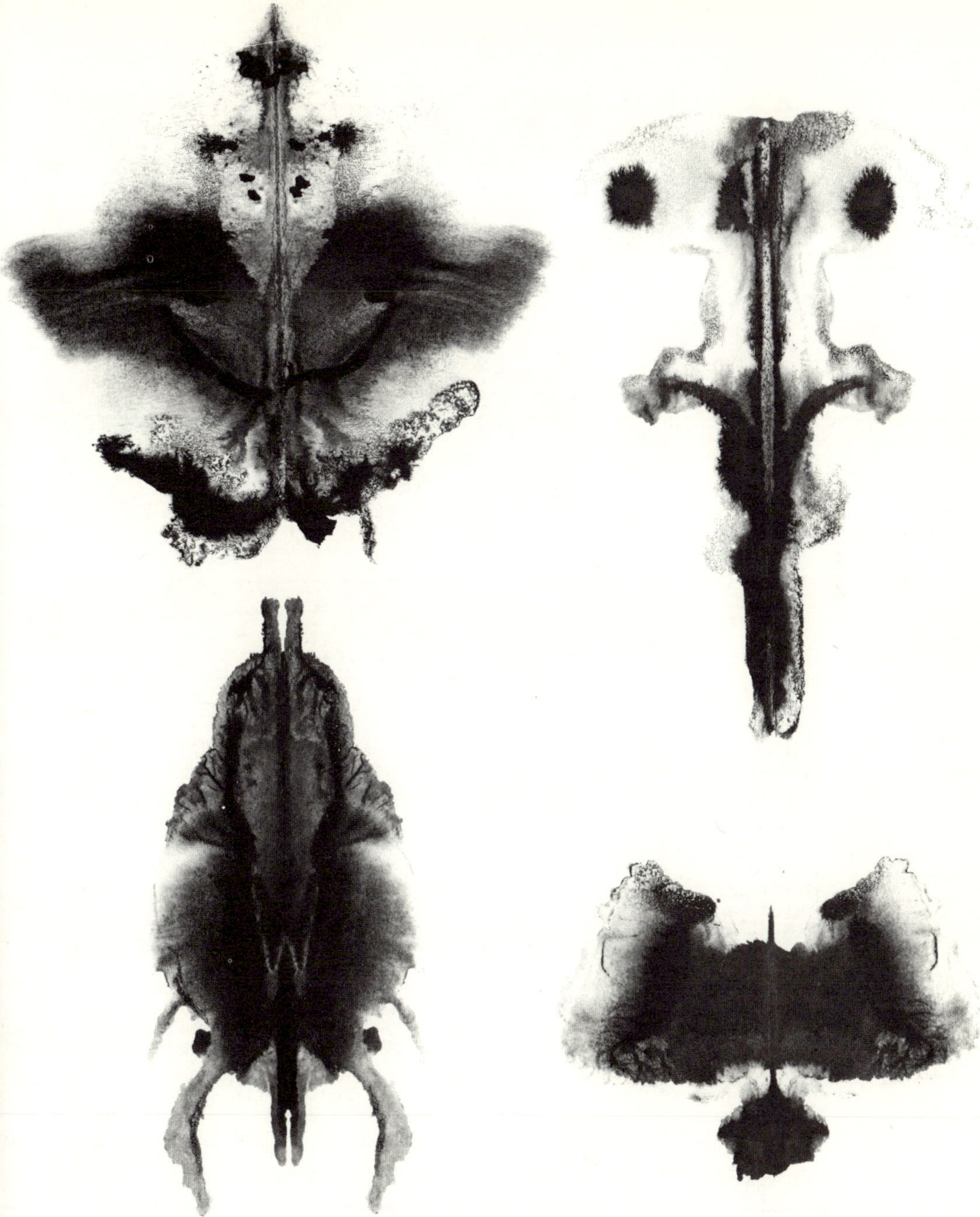

Ask him to take the rorschach ink blot test. It will help you to find out more about his innermost feelings. If he associates all four shapes with the face of George Washington, be on your guard. He may be emotionally attached to your dollar bills.

Picture preference test reveals his compulsions. Napoleon is symbolic of a deep-seated Grandiose Complex often found among psychoanalysts. Choice of the famous painting of "Whistler's Mother" indicates an unresolved Oedipus Complex. And last, but not least, preoccupation with the maze suggests the ubiquitous presence of the most complex of all psychological complexes: the Complex-Complex.*

* If unchecked, this may develop into a more advanced neurological disorder: The Complex-Complex-Complex.

Apperception Test provides information about his formal education. Ask him which of the following mountains the above photograph brings to his mind.

- ☐ Mount Kilimanjaro
- ☐ Mount Kashtan Tau
- ☐ Mount Everest
- ☐ Mount Rainier

A check in any of the boxes shows a thorough knowledge of geography, but not social sciences.

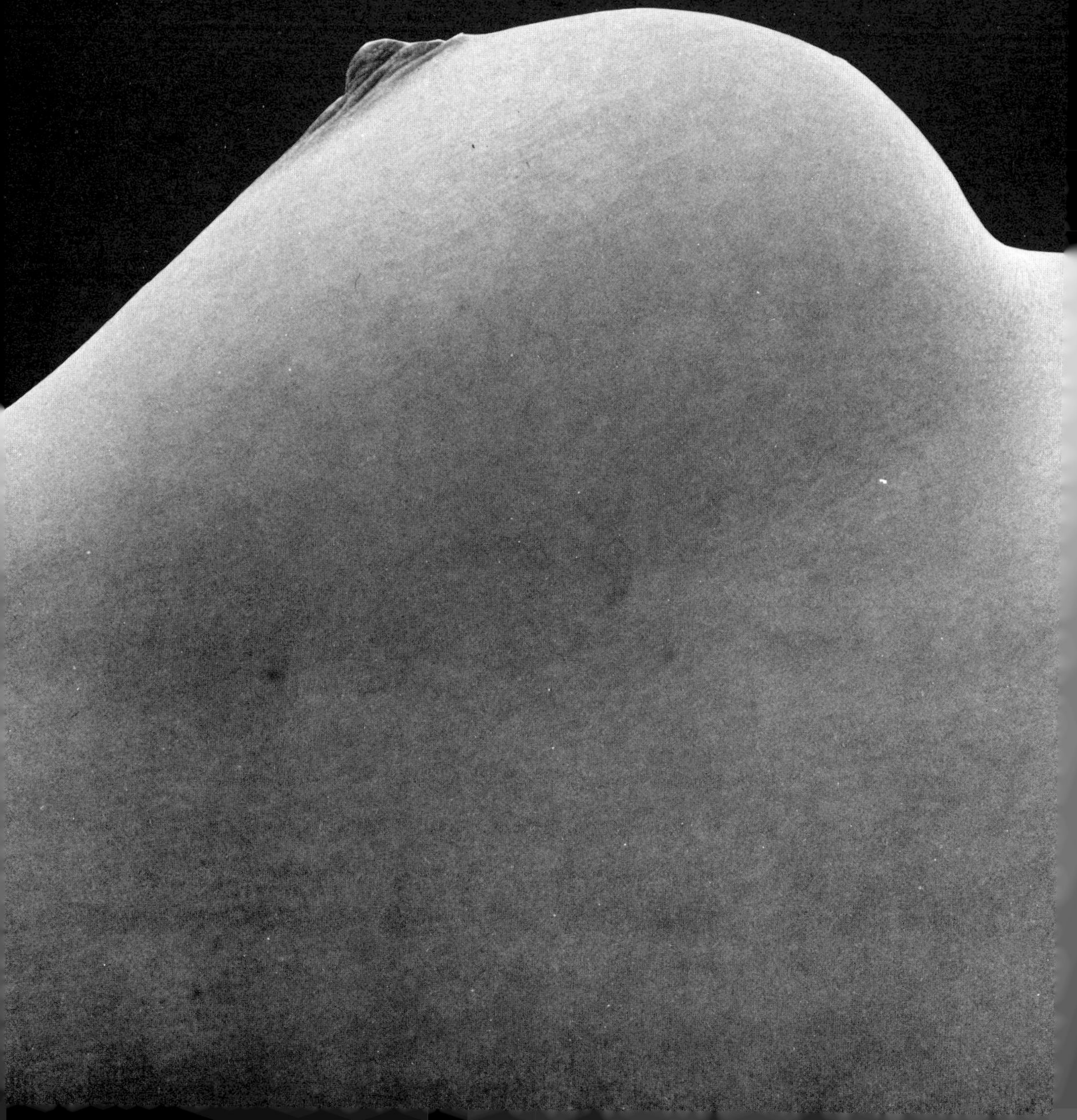

Your first visit will undoubtedly be interrupted by the frequent ringing of the telephone. Don't let the noise upset you. Psychoanalysts are much-sought-after personages; you can't expect them to devote their entire time to one patient only. Listen to his phone conversations; they will show how he handles everyday social situations.

CALLER:	PSYCHOANALYST'S RESPONSE:
MOTHER	"Hello, dear."
WIFE	"What do you want?"
PROSPECTIVE PATIENT	"Please, tell me more about it."
REGULAR PATIENT	"How many times do I have to tell you not to call while I am in conference?"
HIS PSYCHOANALYST	"I am so glad you called, Alfred."
MISTRESS	"Of course, my pet."
INTERNAL REVENUE AGENT	"Last year my expenses exceeded my income."
BROKER	"Get me five hundred more shares."
CLEANING WOMAN	"You are getting me all upset, lady. I found specks of dirt under the couch yesterday."
LIQUOR STORE	"Send up two bottles of bourbon. Hurry!"
UPHOLSTERER	"No, not the couch. My chair!"
HIS WIFE'S ANALYST	"In my professional opinion, you're wasting your time, Doctor. She is a neurotic, you know."

A look at your psychoanalyst's first name should be part of your investigation. All accredited psychoanalysts go under one (or several) of the following Christian (or Jewish) names:

Abraham
Albert
Archibald

Bartholomew
Baruch
Basil
Burgess

Casper
Cecil
Conrad
Cosmo

Dante
Driscoll
Dudley
Dwight

Ebenezer
Eberhardt
Edgar
Egbert
Ellison
Emmanuel
Ezekiel
Ezra

Fabian
Felix
Francis
Fritz

Gasper
Gaylord
Gideon
Gilbert
Gustav
Guthrie

Hamilton
Hans
Harcourt
Hector
Herman
Hubert

Irving
Isaac
Isidore
Ivan

Jeremiah
Job
Jonah
Jonas
Joshua

Konrad

Lazarus
Leopold
Lester
Ludovick

Maurice
Maximillian
Milton
Morgan
Moses

Nathaniel
Nicholas
Norman

Oakley
Ormund
Oscar
Otto

Philip

Quincey

Reginald
Reuben
Rudolph
Rupert

Samuel
Saul
Sebastian
Seymour
Sherman
Sidney
Sigfrid
Sigmund*
Solomon
Sylvester

Theodore
Tobias

Uriah

Valentine
Victor
Vincent

Walter
Webster
Wilfred
Winifred
Winthrop
Wyatt

Zachariah
Zebulon
Zeke

*He may be a name-dropper.

Examine his surroundings, especially his couch. Test it for size and comfort. Its length should cover the distance between the top of your head **(A)** and the tip of your toe **(B)** as the crow **(C)** flies. The mattress **(D)** should be firm enough to hold your weight but not so much that it interferes with your sleeping schedule.

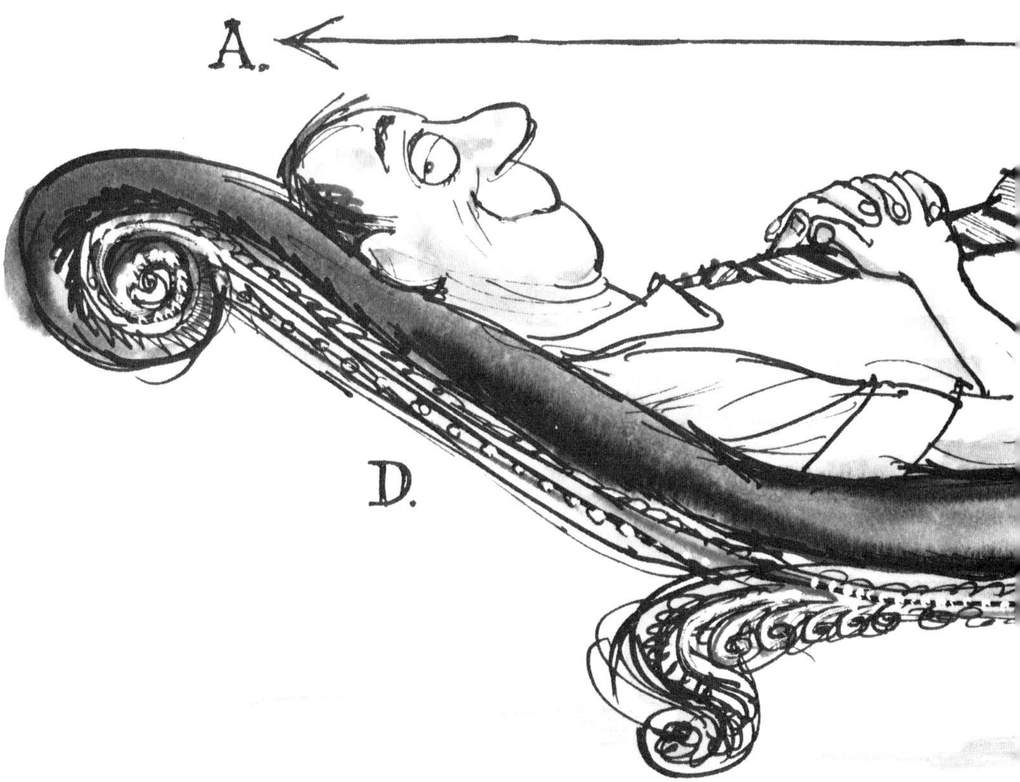

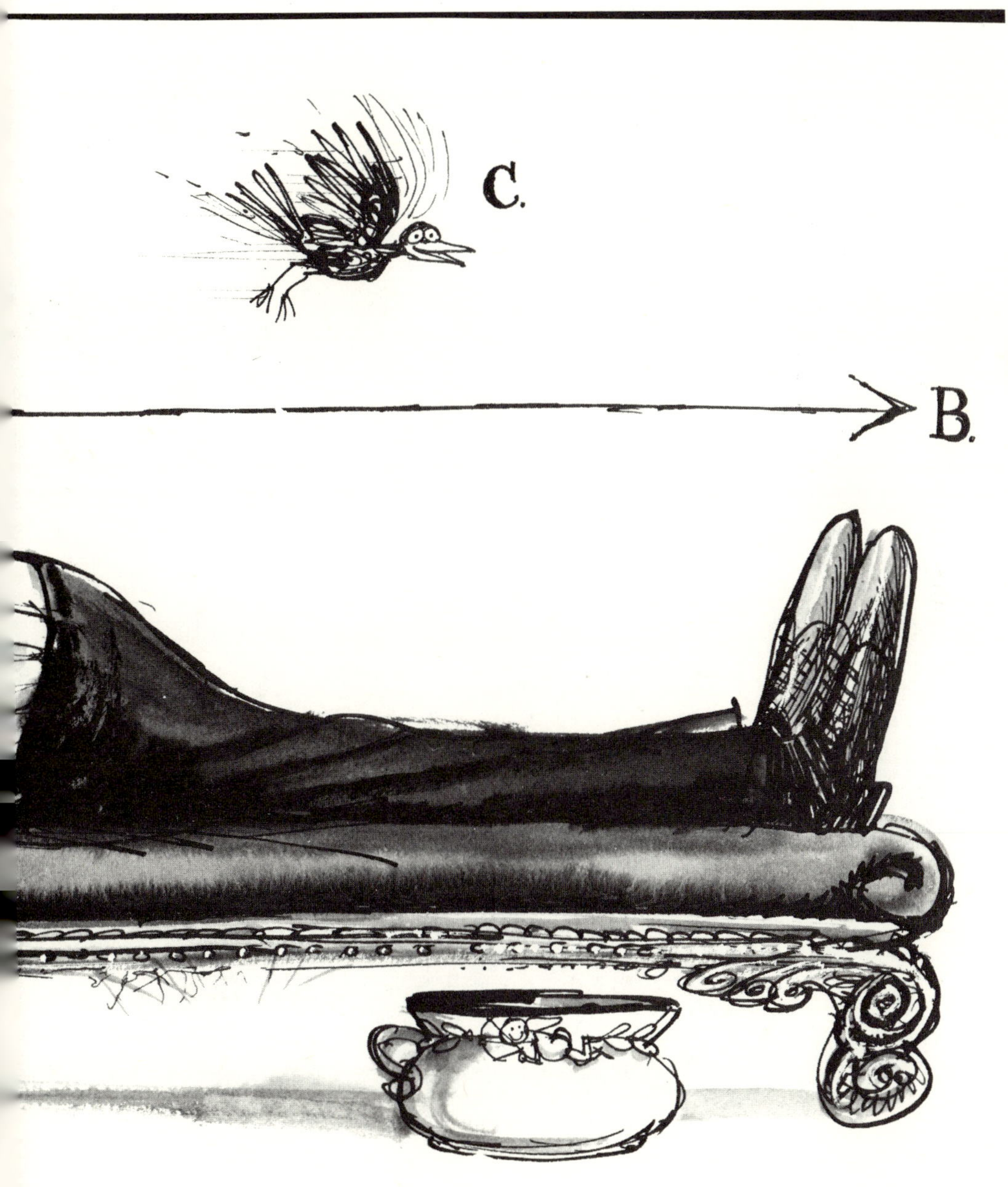
C.
B.

The most reliable source of information about your psychoanalyst is his patients, of course. You'll meet them in the waiting room.

2

GETTING OFF TO A GOOD START WITH YOUR NEUROTIC PSYCHOANALYST

The initial stage of your analysis—say, the first five to ten years—is important, for it is during this period that your analyst gathers his quick first impressions of you. They will stay with him unchanged for years to come, since it goes against his professional judgment to be wrong about anything.

You must do everything you can to make your analyst feel right at home from the very first time you see him. Keep in mind that all psychoanalysts are basically shy, insecure persons who would vastly prefer to be left alone, if they only could make this economically feasible. Your appearance in his office time after time is a constant source of irritation to him. Your stopping off on his finest—and only—couch in the office upon arrival, and your insistence to talk about your day instead of his, does not in the least alter his opinion of you.

Once you learn to appreciate his feelings, it will be easier for you to understand his reaction to you; i.e., his moving his chair across the room as you take your position on the couch, and well out of your range of vision. This is simply his way of preventing you from interfering with his extracurricular activities during analysis, such as his making phone calls, shaving, picking his nose, mending his socks, humming to himself, tapping on the floor, fingerpainting on the wall, playing jacks, taking his midday siesta in the morning, afternoon, evening, or late at night.

You will also understand why your psychoanalyst should lock himself into the coat closet, taking with him a book, food, water, and other provisions.

In order to pass time even faster, psychoanalysts invented a Daylight Saving Time System different from any other used by anyone. Theirs does away with the sixty-minute hour, substituting forty-five minutes in place of it. This makes it possible for analysts to complete an eight-hour working day in six hours—a truly remarkable feat, considering that they bill by the hour.

ARRIVING AT THE OFFICE

STARTING THE SESSION

ON THE COUCH

STILL ON THE COUCH

ENDING THE SESSION

LEAVING THE OFFICE

Keep smiling at all times. This will go a long way in helping to alleviate the sense of despair which envelops him upon seeing you.

The manner in which you greet or bid him farewell, profoundly affects the mood of your psychoanalyst. Choose your words carefully.

WHEN YOU ENTER HIS OFFICE, DON'T JUST STAND THERE AND SAY:	WHEN YOU EXIT HIS OFFICE, DON'T JUST STAND THERE AND SAY:
"HELLO"	"GOOD BY"
SAY:	**SAY:**
"WHAT A BEAUTIFUL DAY."	"I HAD A PERFECTLY MARVELOUS TIME, DOCTOR."
"MY, MY, YOU LOOK TIRED, DOCTOR. WOULD YOU WANT ME TO COME BACK SOME OTHER TIME?"	"LET'S KEEP IN TOUCH, EH?"
"AND WHAT HAVE WE GOT TO TALK ABOUT TODAY?"	"I CAN HARDLY WAIT TO HEAR THE END OF YOUR STORY AT OUR NEXT SESSION."
"HERE I COME!"	"HERE I GO!"
"AND HOW'S YOUR MOM?"	"GIVE MY REGARDS TO YOUR MOM."
"EVERYTHING ALL RIGHT AT HOME?"	"CALL ME* IF YOU GET LONELY."

* But not after 3 A.M.

If he appreciates music and you play a musical instrument, bring it along to your next session.

A few drinks—five or six—may help to ease his tensions.

Nine ways to cheer up your analyst:

DRY MARTINI

1 part French (dry) vermouth, 4 parts gin or vodka. Stir with cracked ice until cold. Strain, serve in pre-chilled cocktail glass with green olive, cocktail onion, or a twist of lemon peel.

RYE HIGHBALL

1 cube of ice, 2 oz. Old Mr. Boston Rye Whiskey. Fill 8-oz. highball glass with ginger ale or carbonated water. Add twist of lemon peel, if desired, and stir.

SCOTCH WHISKEY HIGHBALL

1 cube of ice, 2 oz. scotch whiskey. Fill 8-oz. highball glass with ginger ale or carbonated water. Add twist of lemon peel, if desired, and stir.

WHISKEY SOUR

½ jigger lemon juice, 1 teaspoon sugar, 1 jigger (1½ oz.) bourbon or rye. Shake well with cracked ice, strain into glass. Serve with orange slice on rim of glass, and cherry.

BLOODY MARY COCKTAIL

1½ oz. vodka, 1½ oz. tomato juice, 1 dash lemon juice. Shake well with cracked ice and strain into Old Fashioned cocktail glass with cube of ice.

GIN AND TONIC

2 oz. dry gin, cube of ice. Fill glass with quinine water and stir. Use 12-oz. Tom Collins glass.

HOT BUTTERED RUM

Put lump of sugar into hot whiskey glass and fill two thirds with boiling water. Add square of butter and 2 oz. rum. Stir and grate nutmeg on top.

IRISH COFFEE

Into a pre-warmed 8-oz. stemmed glass (or coffee cup), pour 1½ oz. irish whiskey. Add 1 or 2 teaspoons sugar and fill to within ½ inch of top with strong, very hot black coffee. Stir to dissolve sugar. Float to brim with chilled whipped cream. Do not stir. Drink through floating cream.

SPECIAL DRINK FOR A HANGOVER

Fill up a glass with water. Add a slice of Alka-Seltzer and watch it fizz. Stir well. Force your analyst's mouth open by holding his nose and pour contents down his throat.

In order for you to cope with your analyst's emotional problems and assure his, if not your, continuous progress, you must have at least a cursory understanding of psychoanalysis.

The origin of psychoanalysis goes back a long way. In fact, its tenets were already known in Biblical times by a fair maiden who—bored by her daily routine—persuaded her boy friend to share an apple with her. His name was Adam, and he was the first neurotic on record.

Millions of other neurotics followed him and it became obvious that someone had to invent psychoanalysis.

The inventor's name was Sigmund Freud. He discovered, mostly through listening to his wife, that people rarely said what they thought; instead, they said what they _thought_ they thought.

He also learned that neurotics talked a great deal when positioned horizontally.

In fact, they were so anxious to talk in this position that they agreed to pay substantial fees just to be heard. So Freud put a couch in his office and made way for modern psychotherapy.

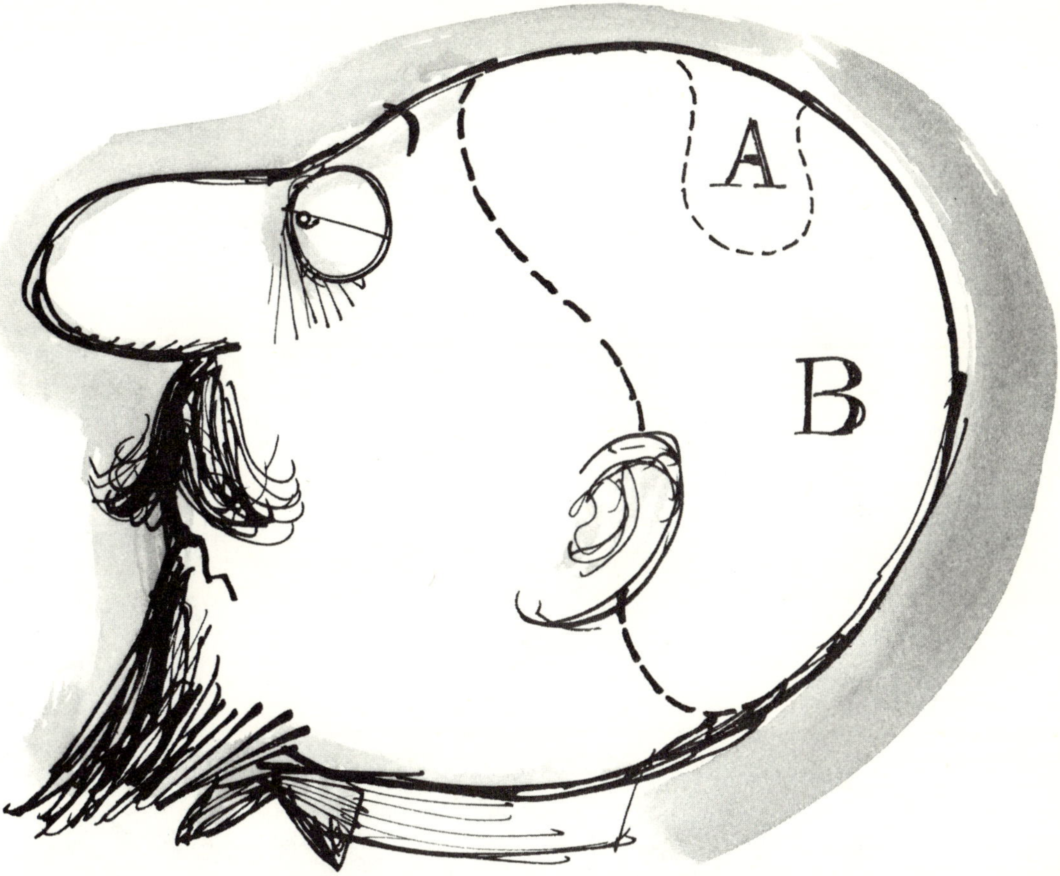

Analyst's psychic apparatus is the same as any other normal neurotic's. It is divided into two major components: **(A)** The small Conscious and **(B)** the larger and more active Subconscious.

Subconscious takes care of such conditioned–but necessary–reflex actions as stroking beard, rocking back and forth in chair, doodling, blinking, frowning, rapping fingers, whistling, mumbling, sucking at pipe, looking out the window, and answering patient's questions. The major function of the Conscious is to send bills at end of each month.

Make your therapist feel at home
by inviting him to use his couch.

3

HOW TO BECOME YOUR NEUROTIC PSYCHOANALYST'S "FATHER IMAGE"

Sooner or later, after your first visit or thereabouts, a significant change takes place in your therapist's attitude. A new and meaningful relationship develops between you and him.

He will start looking up to you as an authority figure.

The phenomenon is known as "the development of a 'father image.'"

It is part of every analysis. Your analyst will greet it as a welcome and familiar sign; he knows exactly how to cope with it. First of all, he will appoint you as "the father." That leaves him with only one other choice; to be your son. As far as he is concerned, this arrangement is just fine, for it gives you a sense of responsibility and, more importantly, it allows him to act like a child.

The search for parental love is not unique to psychoanalysts: All living beings feel that way during their formative years. Psychological studies among captive baby gorillas show that even they get annoyed when left in their cages without their parents.

With his father and mother, a baby gorilla's disposition improves. He now feels part of a family unit.

Deep down, your psychoanalyst's reactions are the same as a baby gorilla's. Left to his own devices by his father and mother at the age of forty-five, your analyst still feels the pangs of early parental rejection. Calling for the next patient, his face reveals his true sentiments.

Close-up of the analyst's face.

The lack of parental affection may cause your analyst to look for "Love Substitutes."
This is an important part of his analysis; he is beginning to manifest a desire to belong.
Do not snatch the pillow away from him.
Let him have the chair.
Leave his ice cream alone.
They belong to him.

When your therapist talks about his childhood, maintain respectful silence. Give him a chance to tell his side of the story; forget about yours. No psychoanalyst ever had a simple childhood or else he would never become a psychoanalyst.

Permit him to act out his early frustrations in the office; it is better for him to do it on the premises rather than on the street where he could be arrested for causing a riot.

After ten years or so, you will note a definite improvement in his behavior. He will start acting his age. He will no longer insist on calling you "daddy." Instead, he will simply address you as "dad."

He will, of course, still depend on you for economic support, but that is all. When this occurs, your attitude toward him should change too. Stop talking down to him as though he were a child.

Go ahead, talk to him at his level. Discuss his friends, the gang, his car, and his dates (if any) with him, if that's what he wants. Most of all, start asking him what he would like to be* when he grows up.

* Encourage him to be a psychoanalyst.

Talk to him as though he were your own son. **Make him feel wanted.**

Read to him his favorite rhymes.

Humpty Dumpty sat on a wall,
Humpty Dumpty had a great fall;
All the King's horses, and all the King's men
Couldn't put Humpty Dumpty together again.

Little Miss Muffet
Sat on a tuffet,
Eating her curds and whey;
There came a big spider,
And sat down beside her,
And frightened Miss Muffet away.

Three blind mice! See how they run!
They all ran after the farmer's wife,
Who cut off their tails with a carving knife,
Did you ever see such a sight in your life
As three blind mice?

Diddle diddle dumpling, my son John
Went to bed with his breeches on,
One stocking off, one stocking on;
Diddle diddle dumpling, my son John.

Hush-a-bye, baby, lie still with thy daddy,
Thy nanny has gone to the mill,
To get some meal to bake a cake,
So, pray, my dear baby, lie still.

Be with him when he needs you.

If you are a female patient, show him maternal love.

What you say to your psychoanalyst makes a lasting impression on him. Treat him as you would your own child.

"NOW DON'T YOU GO DISAPPOINTING ME, DOCTOR."

"I'VE KNOWN ALL ALONG THAT YOU WOULD GROW INTO A FINE, UPSTANDING CITIZEN."

"IT'S GOING TO RAIN TODAY, DON'T FORGET YOUR GALOSHES."

"BUTTON UP YOUR OVERCOAT."

"YOU'VE BEEN SUCH A GOOD BOY TODAY."

"STOP ASKING SO MANY SILLY QUESTIONS."

"JUST FOR THAT, NO TELEVISION FOR YOU ALL DAY TOMORROW."

"I AM GLAD TO SEE THAT YOUR MANNERS ARE IMPROVING."

"GROWN-UP PEOPLE DON'T PICK THEIR NOSES."

"ISN'T IT PAST YOUR BEDTIME?"*

* Psychoanalysts often insist they want to stay up late.

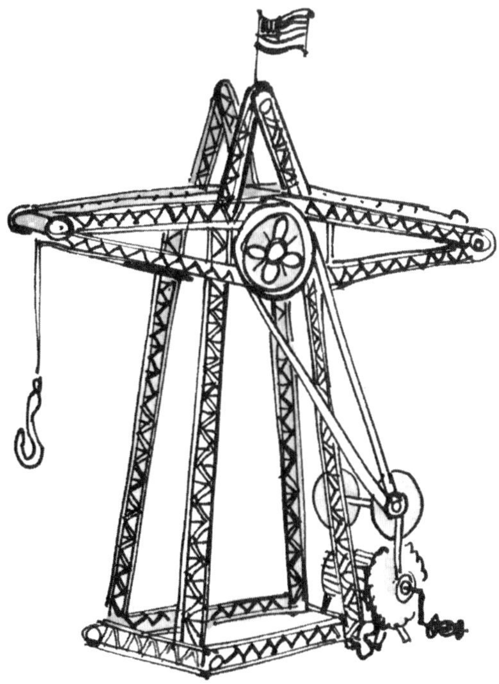

Surprise him with
a present now and then.

For Christmas, give him a <u>real</u> bicycle.

4

HOW TO STAY AWAKE ON YOUR NEUROTIC PSYCHOANALYST'S COUCH

After a few months of analysis, another problem will come up—the most formidable so far.

You will keep falling asleep on the couch.

Stop blaming yourself. It happens to all the patients, except those who are on the couch trying to get rid of chronic insomnia.

There are reasons for your sleepiness. You are in a horizontal position, just like in a bed. Moreover, your analyst tells you to relax. You want to follow his instructions. Besides, you have been looking forward to a catnap all day long. This is your long-awaited opportunity.

This being the case, you must learn either (1) to stay awake or (2) to sleep with your eyes open.

At times, your analyst may stop talking—as, for example, when he is taking a nap. Staying awake under such conditions requires even more self-discipline. It may help you to train your eardrums to respond to noises other than his voice. Audible in a

psychoanalyst's office may be sounds coming from a variety of sources such as **(1)** family upstairs, **(2)** dog, **(3)** dripping faucet, **(4)** patient eager to have his turn on the couch, **(5)** people singing a duet in the waiting room, and **(6)** snoring.

1.
2.

To keep your eyelids from drooping, stare at the ceiling. Observe sights (**1**) cracks, (**2**) housefly, (**3**) spider's web, and (**4**) footprints.

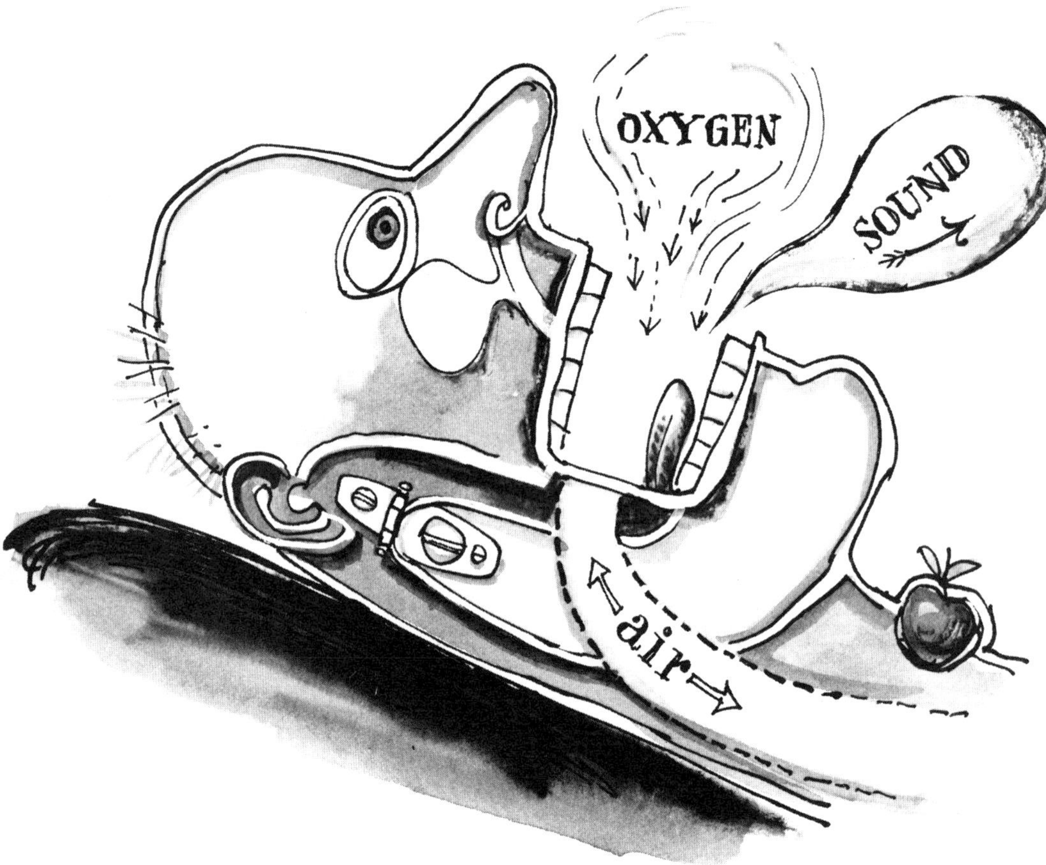

Opening and closing your mouth will help you carry on. Keep talking. Jaw movements demand physical exertion, pumping air into your lungs. This will stimulate blood to flow into your brain.

There will be times, of course, when you will have nothing to say. This should not keep you from talking; it should not even give you a reason for a momentary pause. Talking fluently about absolutely nothing at great length is a skill most patients develop sooner or later; it is as good a way as any to while away one's time.

Once you have mastered the art of free association, your chances of staying awake for the full forty-five minutes improve significantly. Speaking will force you to breathe with regularity, and you can listen to your own voice. For example:

STREAM OF CONSCIOUSNESS: APPLE . . . BALLOON . . .
TWO BALLOONS . . .
WOMAN . . . MAN . . . BED

(Take a deep breath)

STREAM OF CONSCIOUSNESS: BED . . . CHAIR . . . LEGS . . .
A PAIR OF ANKLES . . .
WOMAN . . . MAN . . . BED

(Take a deep breath)

STREAM OF CONSCIOUSNESS: BED . . . FOUR POSTERS . . .
POSTER . . . ART . . .
NUDE . . .
WOMAN . . . MAN . . . BED

(Take a deep breath)

STREAM OF CONSCIOUSNESS: BED . . . SHEET . . .
WHITE . . . VIRGIN . . .
WOMAN . . . MAN . . . BED

(Take a deep breath)

STREAM OF CONSCIOUSNESS: BED . . . PILLOWS . . .
TWO BALLOONS . . .
WOMAN . . . MAN . . . BED

(Take a deep breath.
Now start all over.)

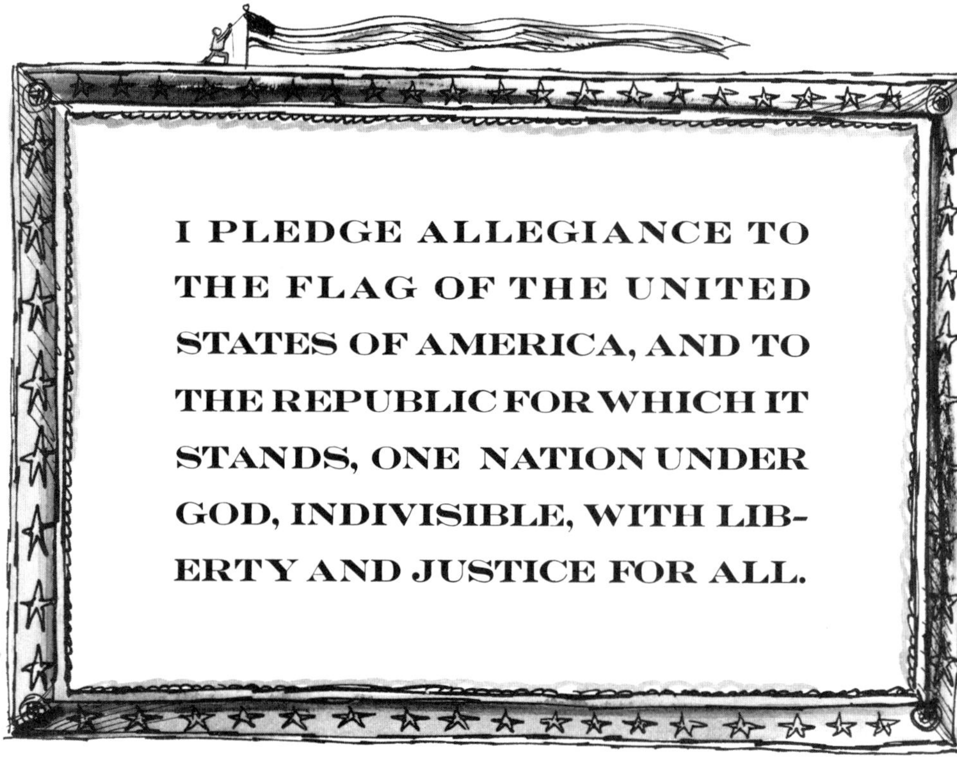

If small talk is beginning to bore you and you feel up to making a more important statement, go ahead. Your analyst won't stop you; he will be impressed by the depth of your thinking.

1, 2, 3, 4, 5, 6, 7, 8, 9, 10, 11, 12, 13, 14, 15,
16, 17, 18, 19, 20, 21, 22, 23, 24, 25, 26, 27,
28, 29, 30, 31, 32, 33, 34, 35, 36, 37, 38, 39,
40, 41, 42, 43, 44, 45, 46, 47, 48, 49, 50.

If you run out of words, use numbers.

Always keep an alarm clock next to the couch. Adjust it to ring every fifteen minutes.

Listen to your favorite radio program.

Or watch a television show.

Keep your body active on the couch. Try isometric exercises.

EXERCISE NO. 1:
Wiggle your toes

EXERCISE NO. 2:
Jiggle your fingers

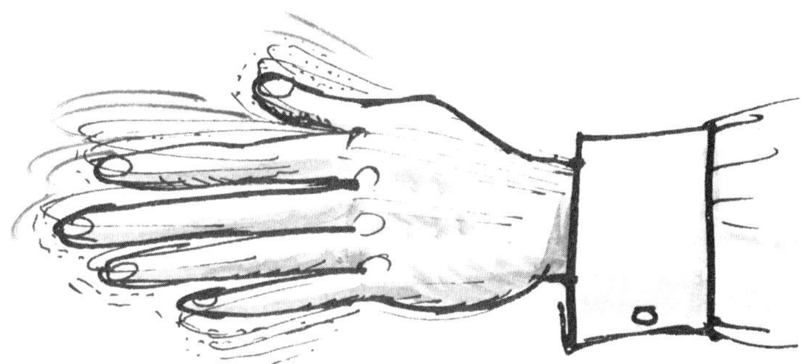

EXERCISE NO. 3:
Twitch your nose

If you must sleep with your eyes shut, make sure your analyst won't notice. Bring your sunglasses to the office.

5

HOW TO KEEP YOUR NEUROTIC PSYCHOANALYST INTERESTED

Psychoanalysts quickly grow bored by the proceedings in their office unless they are allowed to talk freely and without interruption or to busy themselves with some activity other than listening (see Chapter 2, page 16).

As a matter of fact, they have exactly the same problem as you: how to stay awake during analysis.

It is your responsibility to see that your analyst does not fall asleep while you are there. If you cannot keep your eyes open, neither can he.

Remember, it is in your interest to keep things going; you are the one who is paying for being in his office, not he.

Make your money work for you.

If, after the session, the page in your analyst's notebook

looks like this, you apparently lost his interest.

Many patients fail to use their forensic talents in an analyst's office.

They think they have an audience that is easily amused. They show up at sessions without notes or even an outline of their speech. They rely completely on their ability to improvise.

No wonder their analysts fall asleep.

You must learn to make your analyst listen to you. Remember, he is not as interested in your story as he is in catching up on his sleep.

Always speak from your diaphragm for better projection. Your voice must be strong enough to carry across the room where he sits facing the wall. And if, by any chance, he is awake, your voice must overpower his.

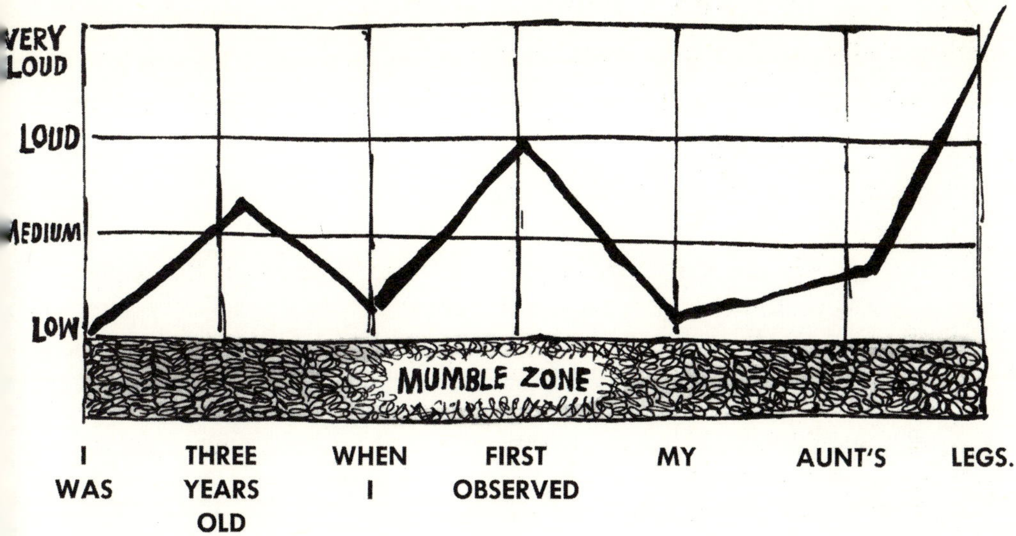

Avoid speaking in a monotonous voice. Vary your pitch for emphasis.

Accompany your speech with a variety of animated expressions.

Open your talk with a humorous remark. This will put your analyst at ease. He may even crack a smile. Listed below are a few jokes that will help you in establishing a congenial atmosphere in the office.

Some people call it the Drinking Man's Diet. Some call it the Air Force Diet. Either way you end up flying.

I can't understand why we're having all this trouble with France. Let's face it, the French and Americans have always had the same interests – broads! . . . I don't blame the West for being shook. I've always considered France the Texas of Europe – where never is heard a discouraging word . . . Here's an entire country dedicated to the proposition – and suddenly they're saying no!

Last year Americans smoked six hundred billion cigarettes! Six hundred billion! Do you realize if you placed those six hundred billion cigarettes end to end, lit the first one, and took a drag on the last one – you might have a filter that works?

I may look healthy, but under all this tan, you should know how pale I am!

And so we come to my favorite Christmas story – the one about the Russian named Rudolph who looked out of his Moscow window and said: "It's raining." His wife looked up from her knitting and disagreed: "It's snowing." Whereupon Rudolph went into a tantrum: "It's raining, dammit! I said it's raining – and Rudolph the Red knows rain, dear!"

So this crook went up to the cashier in a Chinese restaurant, pulled out a gun and said: "Gimme $200 in fives, tens, and twenties – to go!"

Do you realize it only took six days to create the world? Just shows you what can be done if you don't take coffee breaks!

This three-star general was talking to his aide: "You say we've made the greatest blunder in the history of aviation? It's the first rocket you've ever seen that can only fly sideways? Well I guess there's only one thing left to do – stamp it TOP SECRET and file.

Use visual aids to dramatize the highlights of your presentation.

Only self-centered patients talk about their own trivial experiences all the time. Widen your discussion by bringing up subjects of general interest:

THE DIGESTIVE SYSTEM OF A GOLDFISH

THE DECLINE OF THE ROMAN EMPIRE

NOISE CONTROL AT MUNICIPAL AIRPORTS

THE URBAN CRISIS

THE CIRCUITRY OF AN ELECTRONIC COMPUTER

REPAIRING A CYCLOTRON

DEFICIT SPENDING IN GOVERNMENT

THE TALKING MECHANISM OF A PORPOISE

JAPANESE POSTER ART

PRESBYOPIA

GESTALT PHILOSOPHY

THE URGENT CASE OF SOCIAL INVESTMENT

THE ANARCHY OF THE MEGALOPOLIS

THE COST OF SPACE DISCOVERY

TARIFF POLICY AND INCREASING FOREIGN COMPETITION

AGRICULTURAL SUBSIDIES AND THE INDUSTRIAL FARM

THE AVERAGE INCOME OF PSYCHOANALYSTS

Learn to have dreams interesting enough to warrant your analyst's attention.

I was holding an important business conference in the nude.

I was a commuting centaur.

I was having a drink with a crocodile.

I was the head of a large family.

Certain words—in or out of context—will make your psychoanalyst take sudden interest. Use them. Here are a few:

SEX	SEXUAL RELATIONS
SEXY	SEXUAL
SEXOLOGY	BISEXUAL
SEXY SEXOLOGIST	HETEROSEXUAL
OVERSEXED	HOMOSEXUAL
BODILY APPETITE	POLLINATION
BIOLOGICAL URGE	IMPREGNATION
CARNAL DESIRE	GESTATION
GENITALS	SPERM
VULVA	MASCULINE
WOMB	FEMININE
PENIS	OVUM
PROCREATION	LECHERY
COPULATION	SEDUCTION
SEXUAL CONGRESS	DEFLORATION
SEXUAL UNION	RAPE

If your analyst has an ear for music, put in tune your stream of consciousness. (To be sung to the tune of "Believe Me, If All Those Endearing Young Charms.")

**Jump up and down on the couch if—
in spite of all your efforts—
your psychoanalyst still
keeps falling asleep.**

6

HOW TO HELP YOUR NEUROTIC PSYCHOANALYST OVERCOME HIS FEELINGS OF INADEQUACY

Many psychoanalysts feel inadequate.

This is understandable when one considers that many analysts are inadequate.

There also may be another, more deep-seated reason for his feeling that way.

It could be that his patients are at fault. During sessions, the analyst's own neurosis—his pride and joy—is often being challenged by those who have phobias, fixations, obsessions, manias, and a collection of childhood traumas of their own. Insistence that these are a match for his own leaves the analyst unsure of the basis of his neurosis.

Hence, his feeling of inadequacy.

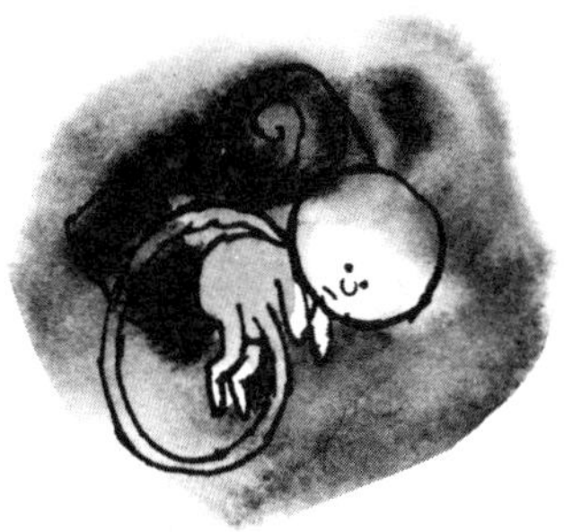

FIRST MONTH

THIRD MONTH

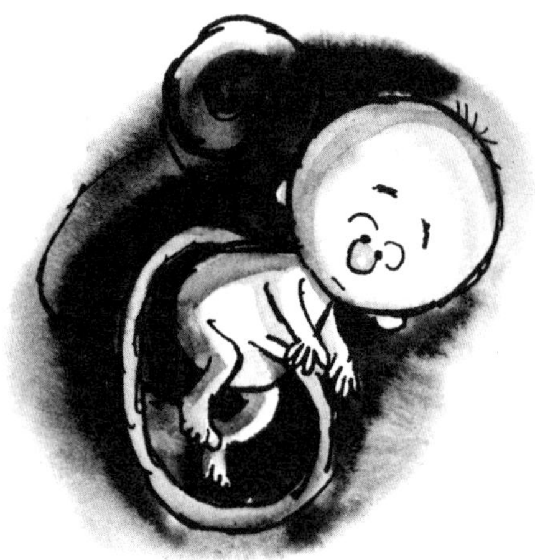

FIFTH MONTH

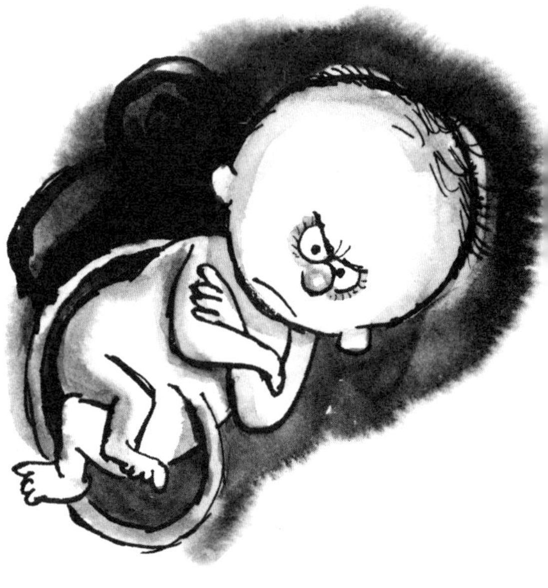

NINTH MONTH

The analyst's feelings of inadequacy began even before birth. Cooped up in his mother's womb for nine months with hardly a chance to ever go outside, he had time to think. And he could not help noticing that his appearance was nothing like what is normally expected of a human being.

At his arrival, he was humiliated in public by a slap on the buttock.

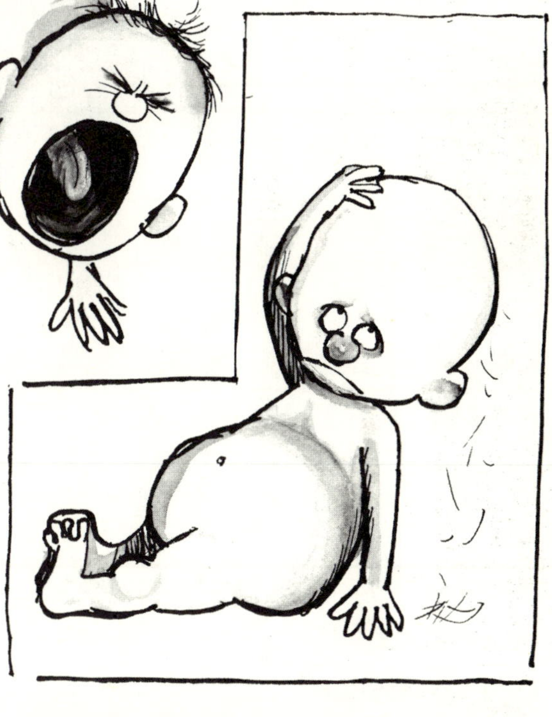

After the first few weeks, he became prematurely bald.

For years, everybody looked down at him.

He couldn't even keep up with his father.

He was not allowed to see the most interesting movies.

He couldn't grow a beard.

Throughout his childhood, his father was always one up on him. He got only the second choice.

HIS FATHER HAD:	HE HAD:
BANK BOOK	PIGGY BANK
PLAYBOY MAGAZINE	JACK AND JILL
AUTOMOBILE	BICYCLE
CIGAR	BUBBLE GUM
BOURBON	CHOCOLATE SODA
12 NECKTIES	1 NECKTIE
RIFLE	WATER PISTOL
SENIOR CLUB MEMBERSHIP	JUNIOR CLUB MEMBERSHIP
LONG FORM TAX RETURN	SHORT FORM TAX RETURN
CREDIT CARDS	BASEBALL TRADING CARDS
INDIGESTION	TUMMY-ACHE
DOUBLE BED	BUNK BED

And now that the psychoanalyst has reached adulthood, he cannot even keep up with his own child.

Naturally, his traumatic childhood left your analyst on the verge of total collapse. Do not underestimate the impact of his early years. Do not compare his to your own. Avoid dialogues such as the following:

PSYCHOANALYST: I remember my family. It was a large, happy group of people. My parents got along fine . . . they were married for over fifty years. And yet, underneath . . .

PATIENT: My father was a confirmed alcoholic who . . .

PSYCHOANALYST: . . . there were currents of hostility between my parents and the children. All six of us. It's not that they resented me . . .

PATIENT: . . . when my father returned from one of his drinking bouts late at night, he would pick up a chair . . .

PSYCHOANALYST: . . . but I resented them because they wouldn't resent me. Pretending to love me like a brother, they were trying to make me think I was going through a normal childhood. But I wasn't about to be fooled by anyone. My parents wanted me to get a good education . . .

PATIENT: . . . and break it over my mother's head.

PSYCHOANALYST: . . . but I saw right through their scheme. They were trying to demonstrate their love for me by offering material support. I said nothing . . . I accepted everything . . . until one day . . .

PATIENT: When I was three years old, father beat up mother for the last time. When she got up off the floor, she called the police, but when they arrived . . .

PSYCHOANALYST: . . . I let them have it. I gave them a piece of my mind. I told them: They were trying to buy my love. First, they didn't understand what I was getting at . . . you know, the generation gap . . . they just stood there, dumbfounded . . .

PATIENT: . . . he was not there. He left home and that was the last we saw of him.

PSYCHOANALYST: . . . but then the truth slowly dawned upon them. They apologized for their failure to understand me. I couldn't believe my ears. Imagine, apologizing! Apparently, they were trying to give me a guilt complex for the rest of my life!

PATIENT: So my mother had to go to work and I was left in the care of a friendly neighbor.

PSYCHOANALYST: That settled it. I decided to become self-sufficient and accept nothing from my parents beyond their total financial support.

PATIENT: Then, in my fifth year, my mother disappeared and I was . . .

PSYCHOANALYST: Sorry, our time is up. We shall continue our analysis the day after tomorrow. Next patient!

YOU ARE GREAT, YOU ARE GREAT, YOU ARE GREAT, YOU ARE GREAT, YOU ARE GREAT, YOU ARE GREAT, YOU ARE GREAT, YOU ARE GREAT, YOU ARE GREAT, YOU ARE GREAT, YOU ARE GREAT, YOU ARE GREAT, YOU ARE GREAT, YOU ARE GREAT, YOU ARE GREAT.

Help your psychoanalyst to regain his self-confidence.

Occasionally, your analyst will get up from his chair, open the window, look down at the street several stories below, bid you farewell, step over the window sill, and sit down on the outside ledge.

Do not be alarmed. Remember, he is your psychoanalyst and you have his respect. Just call the police and fire department, the mayor, his mother, his psychoanalyst. Do not accept his alibi that he is out there merely to get some fresh air.* Talk softly to him until help arrives. Then go ahead and scream.

* There is no fresh air in a city.

Encourage him to take up a hobby.

Play cards with him. Make sure he wins every time.

Actually, your analyst's feelings of inadequacy may all go back to one thing: his relationship with the opposite sex.

Now that he is approaching middle age, he may have doubts about his masculinity. He may feel, for example, that the time has come when he should start having sexual relations with women.

If this is the case, it is your responsibility to enlighten him about the facts of life. Remember, he had a very busy youth, working hard to become a psychoanalyst; he had no time for girls.

True, in medical school he was given an opportunity to study female anatomy through such devices as human skeletons, drawings, and X rays, but this provided him with only an academic insight.

Presently, having listened to his patients' opinions about sex, he became even more confused about the subject.

It is up to you to set him straight.

To encourage his interest in the opposite sex, bring a few girls to his office.

7

HOW TO DEAL WITH YOUR NEUROTIC PSYCHOANALYST'S TEMPER TANTRUMS

There will be times when your analyst may appear perfectly calm. Don't be misled by appearances. This is only a ruse on his part; he is trying to demonstrate his power of self-control to you.

Underneath the calm exterior, there is a temper ready to explode. Most psychoanalysts feel put out for at least forty-five minutes per session, and for good reason. Even if they move their chairs away from the couch and against the wall, they can't help feeling that you are still there.

Most analysts nurture ambivalent feelings toward their patients, feelings that vacillate between dislike and hate. Between these two extremes, they must make a choice. This is not easy. No wonder that the pressures of indecision leave some therapists with a split personality and, in some cases, with a splitting headache.

Look for subtle—seemingly insignificant—signs of anger. The following clues suggest underlying tensions:

HE PICKS HIS NOSE.

HE SUCKS HIS THUMB.

HE IS TEARING AT HIS HAIR.*

HE LETS OUT A HOWL.

HE ROLLS ON THE FLOOR.

HE BOOS.

HE ATTEMPTS TO SCALE THE WALL.

HE NIBBLES AT THE CARPET.

HE TRIES TO FLY LIKE A BIRD.

HE FOAMS AT THE MOUTH.

HE SWALLOWS HIS CIGARETTES.

HE PUTS THE WASTEBASKET OVER HIS HEAD.

HE CRAWLS UNDER HIS CHAIR.

HE JUMPS ON YOUR STOMACH.

HE BITES ON YOUR EAR.

* Or toupee.

In his fits of revenge, your analyst may demonstrate surprising strength.

Do not provoke him by blowing your nose in a red handkerchief.

Don't upset him by showing him up with your happy thoughts:

I AM SO HAPPY.

I FEEL GOOD TODAY.

WHAT A BEAUTIFUL DAY.

EVERYBODY LOVES ME.

I LOVE EVERYBODY.

I HAVE A GREAT WIFE.

LIFE IS WONDERFUL.

HE IS A NICE GUY.

SHE IS A NICE GIRL.

I GOT A RAISE.

I ENJOY GOING HOME IN THE EVENINGS.

THIS IS A LAND OF OPPORTUNITY.

I BROKE NINETY ON THE GOLF COURSE LAST WEEKEND.

I AM LOOKING FORWARD TO MY FUTURE.

IT IS BETTER TO GIVE THAN TO RECEIVE.

To calm his nerves, color his office green.

JAN.

Give him a massage.

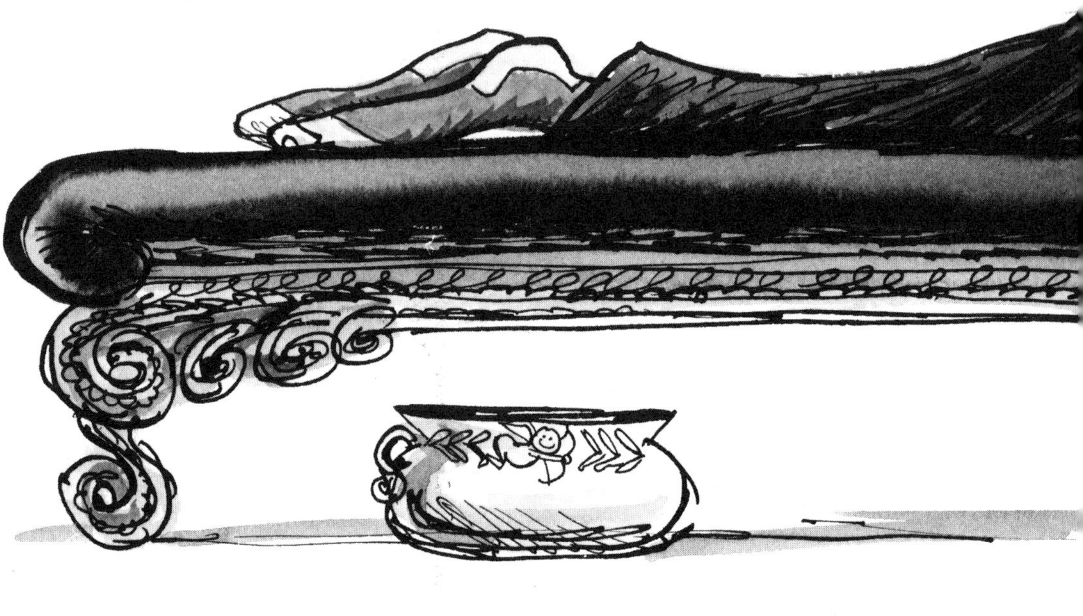

During analysis, everyone should be encouraged to act out his inner conflicts, including your therapist. If there is bodily contact, make it a clean fight. Learn to wrestle. Be gentle with him, however; remember, he is only being playful.

WRISTLOCK

TOEHOLD

LEG SPREAD

HEAD SCISSORS

ARM AND LEG HOLD

HALF NELSON

FULL NELSON

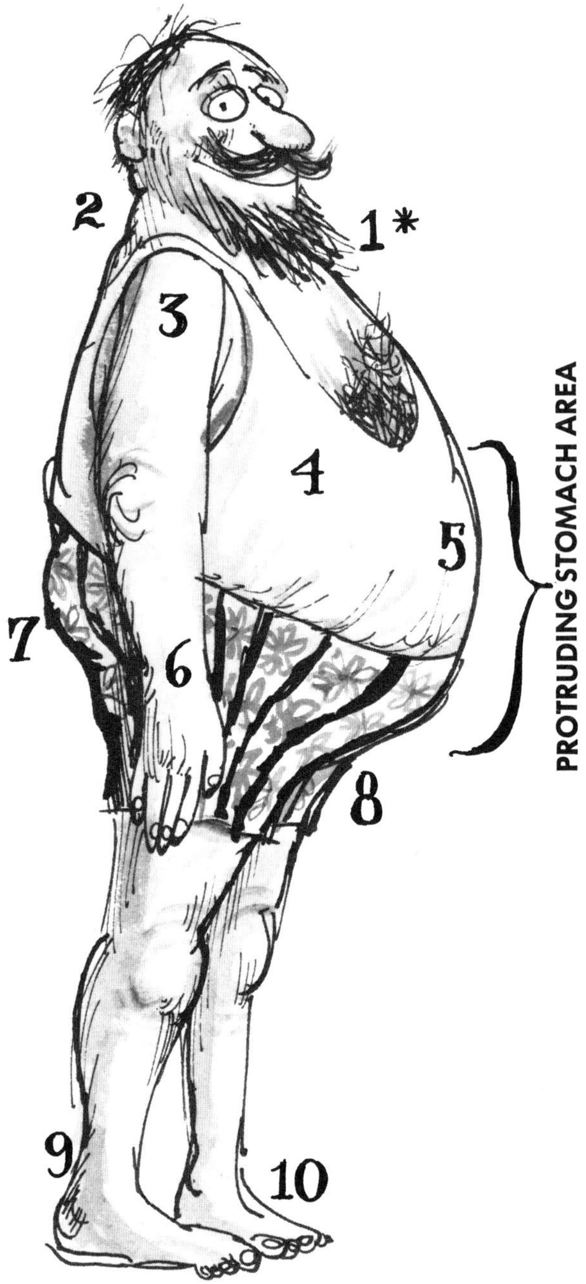

1. **ADAM'S APPLE***
2. **TENDON RUNNING DOWN FROM THE EAR**
3. **NERVES OF THE UPPER ARM**
4. **LIVER**
5. **SOLAR PLEXUS**
6. **WRIST BONES**
7. **TAIL BONE (COCCYS)**
8. **GROIN**
9. **ACHILLES' HEEL**
10. **ANKLE**

*Hidden under his beard.

If you're a judo expert and there seems to be no other way to stop him, try a few well-directed blows at certain parts of his body.

If he keeps resisting, grab hold of his beard.

If everything else fails, come to your next session fully protected.

8

HOW TO LEAVE YOUR NEUROTIC PSYCHOANALYST WITHOUT HURTING HIS FEELINGS

It is relatively easy to decide when to terminate an analysis; i.e., the day you run out of money.

It is more difficult to determine the way you should accomplish this feat.

By now, he probably has gotten used to seeing you and, unconsciously, may even look forward to your appearances. In fact, he may have developed an emotional attachment to you and, particularly, your monthly payments. To bring such a profound and meaningful relationship to an abrupt end requires utmost diplomacy on your part.

You must prepare him first to accept the idea of your leaving him. The best time to tell him about your intentions is sometime at the beginning of the analysis, say, the second or third session.

The following ten or twenty years will give your analyst enough time to absorb the full impact of the news.

Be careful what you tell him. Avoid any suggestion that *you* no longer need *him.* This will only intensify his feelings of rejection and almost surely invite physical violence. It is better to imply that it is he *who* no longer needs *you.*

Expect to listen to his arguments trying to convince you that you are not ready for terminating the analysis. For contrast, he may cite case histories of patients who spent forty or fifty years in analysis, and left only when their voices began to crack and retirement checks were no longer sufficient to cover the cost of their therapy.

He may also tell you that the shortage of time did not allow him to get to know you; in fact, he does not even understand your problem at this point.

Listen to what he has to say.

Do not snore while he talks; at times like this, it is more important than ever not to offend your analyst.

Cape and overalls make thoughtful gifts. Tell him the "S" stands for self-confidence.

Ask his close friends and relatives to help you convince him that he will be able to go on without you.

HIS MOTHER

HIS PSYCHOANALYST

HIS PATIENTS

If your analyst keeps insisting that it is you–not he–who requires further treatment, show him what you learned. Display your knowledge of psychological nomenclature.

DON'T SAY:	SAY:
MAD	HOSTILE
OPINION	SUBJECTIVE THINKING
DRUNK	SITUATIONALLY MALADJUSTED PERSONALITY
WORRY	INTERNAL FRUSTRATION
NEED	PSYCHOLOGICAL NEED
NUT	NEUROTIC
LAZINESS	FLIGHT INTO IDLENESS
GIRL WATCHING	VOYEURISM
PUNCH IN THE NOSE	ASSAULTIVE REACTION
PASSIONATE	PSYCHOSEXUAL
HOUSEBROKEN	TOILET-TRAINED
OH, MY ACHING BACK!	OH, MY PSYCHOSOMATIC DISORDER!

IMPORTANT: ALWAYS REFER TO FREUD AS "SIGMUND."

Work out your getaway plan in detail before you embark upon it at the end of your last session. Then . . . go!

1. Lock door securely behind you.
2. Walk around the potted plant in the reception room.
3. Say farewell to the cat.
4. Use side exit.
5. Take freight elevator to the street.
6. Ask doorman to get you a taxi and tell him shrewdly you'll be back soon.
7. Change taxis at the next block to confound pursuers.

Continued next page

8. Leave town.

9

HOW TO FIND THE NEXT NEUROTIC PSYCHOANALYST JUST RIGHT FOR YOU

See First Chapter.